Time Out

Jane Nelsen
H. Stephen Glenn

Dedication

To the self-esteem of all children

Table of Contents

Introduction

Time out is one of the most popular disciplinary methods used in homes and schools. It is often a humiliating and discouraging experience for children. This book explains how time out can be a positive experience that empowers children to use self-control and self-discipline while enhancing their self-esteem.

When we learned that a school using the isolation booths quoted *Positive Discipline* by Jane Nelsen as advocating time out, we knew it was time for clarification. We do suggest time out *when it is implemented in positive ways instead of humiliating ways*.

The purpose of this book is to clarify the difference between the abuses and effective uses of time out. It will explain the difference between positive uses that help the child and humiliating uses that may stop the behavior but hurt the child.

We have to wonder if anyone who uses time out in a forceful (locked up), humiliating way even thinks about the long-range effects on children. Psychologists and teachers who claim time out is effective are defining "effective" only in terms of controlling the child. In this book, we define effective only in terms of the long-range positive effects on the child.

There are many more gems in this book, such as using goal disclosure to help adults and children understand the belief behind their behavior; abuses and effective uses of logical consequences; the importance of *asking*, instead of *telling*; "what" and "how" questions (Chapter 7 includes details on how a high school principal developed an office referral system based on this concept) and going beyond time out to get children involved in solutions.

Please join us in our dream to empower children.

Chapter 1

Time Out: Encouragement or Discouragement?

The words "time out" are familiar to almost every parent and teacher these days. "I put my son in time out until he could behave," one mother says. "I can't get my daughter to *stay* in time out," wails another. A teacher complains that when he asks a student to step outside the classroom door until he can behave better, the student makes funny faces through the window.

What exactly *is* time out? To one frazzled mom, time out means locking her rebellious toddler in his high chair and setting an egg timer, one minute for each year of her child's age. In some schools, time out means a segre-

3

gated desk, a trip to the principal, isolation in a small room or booth, or suspension. For one terrified boy, time out meant standing for half an hour trying to press his nose against a circle drawn high on the wall by his frustrated father. And for some parents and teachers, time out means time away from the group ". . . to think about what you did!"

Can time out really be all these things? What should it be? And what is its purpose, anyway?

Time out can be an encouraging experience that helps misbehaving, discouraged children—and adults—have time to cool off, feel better and change disruptive behavior to constructive behavior. It can be an affirming, loving action that demonstrates faith in a child's ability to gain control and solve her own problems.

Time out can also be a nightmare for a child locked in a booth or other small space, powerless to get out or to change the situation until he has served the amount of time determined by an adult. This nightmare is shared by adults who value basic human rights (even for children) and believe tactics that humiliate and deprive a child of dignity and respect are means that do not justify the end.

Such uses of time out may "work"—punishment sometimes does, at least in the short run. But does the cost to a child's self-esteem justify the practice, especially when it may lead in the end only to retaliation and rebellion?

It can be tremendously frustrating to deal with misbehaving children, whether at home or in school. The newspapers seem to tell us that the incidence of violence in our schools is rising almost daily. Still, confining children to small spaces is a disturbing practice.

When we heard about the isolation booths used in some schools, we felt outraged and sad. We tried to imagine the feelings of a child locked in a booth four feet square with a window too high for many children to see through. As we role played small children we felt scared, abandoned, powerless, shamed and insecure about our basic worth as people. As older children we felt humiliated, angry and revengeful, and thought about dropping out of school, or about how to get even with those who had shamed us.

We thought, "Surely this practice must be limited to only a few schools." Then we read an article called "Hair Raising Discipline" in *Time* magazine (December 3, 1990, page 57) which tells of a boy confined all day for six

5

weeks in a 10-foot by 13-foot isolation room in a Texas school because he refused to cut his seven-inch ponytail. *Time* reports that this child now has nightmares that the walls of the classroom will close in and crush him.

"But that's appalling," we parents cry. "We would never do that to our children!" Is forcibly restraining a child in some time-out spot really all that different? Is our goal to punish, to give ourselves a break from irritating behavior—or to help our children feel and behave better?

What Or Who Is An Extremely Difficult Child?

Advocates of the isolation booth say it is used only for extremely difficult children. Who defines "extremely difficult" and how does that label affect the child? Some teachers may define the slightest irritation as extremely difficult, while other teachers would not consider locking a child in an isolation booth no matter how severe the misbehavior. Some teachers have used the isolation booth for children who displayed the extremely difficult behavior of chewing gum or talking out of turn. Definitions such as these cause us

6

great concern.

Some teachers who use the isolation box justify its use by saying children are given other options first, such as sitting at their desks with their heads down. If that doesn't work, they are asked to sit in a time-out area in the room facing a three-sided box. If that doesn't work, they are locked in the isolation booth.

What Does Effective Mean?

We have often said, "Beware of what works!" when the long-range results are negative. Now we must add, "Beware of what is effective!"

Some teachers and psychologists believe the isolation booth is effective. Effective for what, we wonder, and for whom? Effective for the teacher, or for the child? It may be effective to stop the misbehavior immediately, but what about the long-range effects on the child? When the long-range results are negative, we must "beware of what is effective!" Our motives and goals in dealing with the children entrusted to our care—the beliefs behind our behavior—are always more important than the behavior itself. Time out is a helpful concept when it is implemented in positive ways, but

7

we must learn the difference between encouraging uses of time out, and humiliating uses that may stop a behavior for the moment but hurt the child.

Imagine for a moment that you are a child of any age. Imagine now what you would feel being confined to a small space, locked into a high chair, or otherwise humiliated or isolated. Would the experience encourage you to do better? Or would it crush your self-esteem, make you feel bad and inferior, and give you an incentive for revenge? The healthiest response we have received from adults who have tried this exercise is, "It would give me something to brag about that the only way they could control me is to lock me up." Most adults give responses that range from feeling rebellious and revengeful to feeling like a bad, inferior person. Not one adult has said, "I really felt this would be good for me and provide me with an inner motivation to do better." Some have said, "I might do better out of total fear and at great cost to my self-esteem."

"Surely making my child stay in his room for five minutes isn't that bad," you may be saying. And the answer may depend on the belief behind the act: are you giving your child a chance to feel better and behave more constructively? Or are you simply interested in controlling your child's behavior? And what is really going on in the mind of your child?

The goal of time out, as with everything we do as parents and teachers, should be to help our children grow into capable, healthy human beings. How then do we use time out in a way that is positive, both for us and for our children?

Chapter 2

Criteria for Positive Time Out

Beware of what *works*. Humiliating time out may *work* but it doesn't help children. The isolation booth may *work* to stop misbehavior (after all, what can a child do while locked up in a 4x4x7 foot box?), but what are the long-range results for the child?

The problem with punishment is that it is based on control, and on withholding love and approval. Punitive time out can result in children with low self-esteem, which can express itself in rebellion, revenge, an excessive need for approval, or simply giving up.

Be Aware of What "Really" Works

When a method has really worked with children, they feel empowered with healthy self-esteem and motivation to improve from an inner desire and locus of control (as opposed to control from others), and they develop skills that will help them solve problems and improve behavior.

Adults can empower children in these ways when they understand a few basic principles of human behavior:

1. Dignity and Respect

A basic principle of Adlerian psychology—the philosophy of maintaining dignity and respect for all human beings—must be incorporated before time out can be used as an effective, encouraging experience that helps children, instead of an experience that creates humiliation and loss of dignity and respect.

2. Misbehaving Children are Discouraged Children

Misbehaving children are discouraged children. They need encouragement so they won't feel the need to misbehave—not shame and humiliation to make them feel more discouraged and more motivated to misbehave. This principle and the *Four Mistaken Goals of Misbehavior* and how they relate to time out will be discussed further in Chapter 3.

3. Humiliation and Shame are Not Effective Motivators

Over the last decade, a number of professional organizations concerned with children (such as pediatrics, psychiatry and social welfare) have formally adopted positions in opposition to spanking, paddling or humiliating children in any way. These organizations have paid attention to the research demonstrating that the long-range damage to children far outweighs the immediate advantage of controlling behavior through punishment.

Where did we ever get the crazy idea that to make children do better, we must first make them feel worse? The truth is that children do better when they feel better—not when they are discouraged about themselves. Therefore, *the number one criterion for positive time out is that it be used to help children feel better, not to make them feel worse.*

Setting Up the Number One Criterion for Positive Time Out

Action is always better than reaction; most parents find it difficult to think clearly and calmly when their children are on a rampage! Many parents in parenting classes have the same questions: "How do I control my anger?" "How do I teach my children to control their anger?" "Is anger wrong?" "When the stress piles up and my children choose exactly the wrong moment to push my buttons, how do I keep from exploding?"

We all feel angry from time to time, and many times our anger is understandable or even justified. Sometimes our children's anger is justified, too! But uncontrolled anger can be destructive, and can lead us to do and say things we later regret.

Many therapists encourage adults—and children—to observe and become aware of the symptoms of approaching anger and to use time out as a way of calming down before anger gets out of control. Sometimes we adults need time out far more than our children do!

Positive time out can—and should—be explained before it's actually needed. When everyone is feeling calm, explain to your children that all of us—parents, teachers and children alike—have times when we lose control of our behavior, feel upset or find ourselves in a bad mood. This doesn't mean we *are* bad; it just means that we feel too bad to know what kind of behavior would help us and others. During these times it can be helpful to have a time-out place to sit quietly and wait until we feel better. This is not a time to sit and think about how bad we are, to do work, to write sentences or to do anything else that could be considered punishment or humiliation. This is a time to do whatever we need to do to feel better and to know that the upsetting feelings or bad mood will pass.

Let children know that when they go to the time-out place, *they* can decide when they feel good enough to behave in ways that will be helpful to them and to others. Sometimes it helps to just feel what you feel for awhile. Some people find it helpful to ask themselves,

"What are these feelings trying to teach me?"
Sometimes it's helpful to think happy thoughts
or do something distracting such as read a good
book, listen to music, or take a nap.

Kids Need Appropriate Power in Their Lives

One way to help young people retain positive power when using time out is to invite
them to set a timer to the amount of time they
think it will take them to cool off and feel better. Later we will discuss how positive power
increases when children participate in design-
ing the guidelines for time out. They can be
involved in planning ways to make time out a
positive rather than a negative experience.

Choice Increases Accountability, Responsibility and Self-Esteem

Allowing children the choice to decide
when they are ready to come out of time out is
extremely important to increase their sense of
accountability, responsibility and self-esteem.
They are empowered with a sense of self-control. Adults miss this point—and set them-

selves up for unnecessary power struggles—when they force children into time out, try to make them feel ashamed, and exert control over when they can leave time out.

When time out is structured in a positive way, children can recognize its value and many take responsibility to go on their own when they need it. Some may need a gentle reminder, such as, "Do you think you can behave respectfully, or do you think you need to go to time out until you feel better?" An adult's tone of voice and body language are the key factors that determine if time out will be seen by children as a helpful or punitive experience.

The Time-Out Spot

Where do you send a child for time out? Almost anyplace—a special chair, a child's own room, or a bench on the school playground—will do if the goal is to help a child feel better. Rather than pointing a bony finger and ordering a child to think about how disrespectful she's been, a parent or teacher might say, "How long do you think you'll need to sit in the time out spot before you'll feel better?" or, "Your behavior tells me that you need time out to feel better. You decide when you feel

17

good enough to use the playground again."
Some schools who use a time-out bench in a
positive way call it the happy bench or the feel
good bench.

Time Out Works for Adults, Too!

"This sort of time out would *never* work
for my kid," you may be saying. It might, if
your children can see how well it works for
you. Parents can model using time out for
themselves with dignity and respect.

Barbara's nine-year-old son had come
home an hour late; dinner was cold and, what
was worse, Barbara had been worried sick.
When Rick finally appeared, looking both defiant and guilty, Barbara realized that at that
moment, anger had the upper hand. So she said
to her son, "Rick, I'm glad you're okay—I've
been worried. But right now I'm so upset that
I need to take some time out to calm down
before we discuss what's happened."

Later, when Barbara felt more relaxed
(and when both she and Rick had a chance to
think about what would happen next), she sat
down with her son to find out what had happened, what had caused it, and what ideas each
of them had to resolve the problem.

18

(See more about the "Ask What?" process in Chapter 7.) Although it took a while to come to an agreement, the episode ended with a hug and a smile, and with both Barbara and Rick feeling good about each other.

If Barbara had followed her initial reaction, she would have punished Rick for his disobedience and, perhaps, never have learned what had really happened. By allowing herself to take time out, she calmed down and remembered several important principles from her parenting class.

1. Get into the child's world and check out his or her perceptions.

2. Look for solutions, not blame.

3. Get young people involved in solutions.

4. Maintain dignity and respect at all times.

Many parents and teachers find it much easier to teach the value of positive time out when their children can see how much it helps them.

A Panacea. . .Not!

Time out is not a panacea and is not appropriate for every circumstance. One principal shared that he finds it very effective to take a misbehaving child for a walk as one alternative to time out. He finds that this creates a cooling off period, and helps to build a foundation of trust and good feelings that are necessary before change can take place. A child treated in a caring and respectful manner has less incentive to misbehave.

Too often adults take a short-range view, focusing on stopping that awful behavior *now* without considering the long-range results. Short-range thinking related to misbehavior frequently incorporates punishment. Punishment usually does stop the misbehavior for the moment, but what about the long-range view?

Long-range parenting (and teaching) focuses on what children will learn that will help them long after the immediate crisis has passed. So many adults have been brainwashed with the idea that children have to suffer to learn. They may learn while suffering punishment, but *what* do they learn? The long-range results of punishment, as described in *Positive Discipline*, are that children may feel one or all of the *Four R's of Punishment*:

1. **Resentment**—"This is unfair. I can't trust adults."

2. **Revenge**—"They're winning now, but I'll get even."

3. **Rebellion**—"I'll do just the opposite to prove that I don't have to do it their way."

4. **Retreat** into:

    a. Sneakiness—"I won't get caught next time."

    b. Reduced self-esteem—"I'm a bad person."

Children will learn positive, long-range lessons of self-discipline and responsibility when they feel encouraged, when they feel belonging and significance, and when they feel they have some power over their lives.

Chapter 3

Understanding the Goals of Misbehavior

Whether you're an adult or a child, and whether you're conscious of it or not, there is a reason for everything we do, a belief behind our behavior. And before we can decide on an appropriate course of action, be it time out or some other form of positive discipline, we need to understand what that belief is.

For example, a two-year-old feels dethroned by the birth of a new baby. The two-year-old observes all the time and attention Mom gives the new baby and *believes* "Mom doesn't love me as much as she loves that baby." The truth doesn't matter; the child's behavior will be based on what she believes is true. It is typical for two-year-olds who believe they have been replaced by a new baby to act like babies. This behavior is based on the belief that "Mom will give me more time and attention if I act like the baby."

Dealing with the Belief Behind the Behavior

Mrs. Burton understood the importance of dealing with the belief behind the behavior. Becky, her three-year-old daughter, was feeling dethroned by the birth of a baby brother. Becky had started whining, soiling her pants and asking for a bottle. One evening, after the baby was asleep, Mrs. Burton asked Becky to sit with her at the kitchen table. On the table were four candles.

"Becky," Mrs. Burton said gently, "I want to tell you a story about our family. These candles represent all of us." She picked up a long candle and said, "This is the Mommy candle; this candle is for me." Lighting the candle with the flame from a match, she said, "This flame represents my love." Picking up another long candle, Mrs. Burton continued, "This is the Daddy candle." As she lit the Daddy candle from her own candle, Mrs. Burton continued, "When I met your Daddy I gave

24

him all my love—and I still had all my love left." Becky could see that both candles now had a bright flame.

Mom now picked up a shorter candle and said, "This is the Becky candle; this candle is for you. Did you know that when you were born I gave you all my love?" She used the flame of the Mommy candle to light the Becky candle. "Now you have all my love. Daddy has all love. And I still have all my love left." She then picked up the smallest candle and lit it with the flame from the Mommy candle. "When your baby brother was born, I gave him all my love. But look—you still have all my love, and Daddy has all my love, and I still have all my love left, because that's the way love is. And now look at all the bright light we have in our family from all this love."

Becky gave her mom a big hug. Several days later Mrs. Burton noticed Becky no longer acted like a baby. It appeared that she changed her belief that Mom loved the baby more than her, so she also gave up the behavior that was based on that belief.

Too often we deal with the behavior alone, and fail to recognize the belief behind the behavior. This is similar to putting out fires while ignoring the arsonist who sets them. Yes, parents and teachers must put out the fires; but the fires will stop only when we deal with the arsonist. We need both to deal with misbehavior and to make every effort to understand the belief behind it.

Get Into the Child's World

The primary goal of human beings is to find belonging and significance. Rudolf Dreikurs taught that "a misbehaving child is a discouraged child." Misbehaving children are discouraged because they do not believe they have belonging and significance. When we use time out in a way that punishes and humiliates, children only become more discouraged.

Dreikurs defined four mistaken goals of behavior that children choose—usually unconsciously—when they feel they do not belong or have significance. The goals are *mistaken goals* because a child mistakenly believes this behavior will lead to belonging and significance. The chart on page 41 defines the four mistaken goals of behavior and the belief behind each.

Same Behavior—Different Beliefs

The same behavior—such as neglected homework—could be a result of any of the four goals. A child seeking belonging through *attention* could believe, "If I don't do my homework, you'll pay attention to me and I'll feel special."

A child seeking belonging through *power* may believe, "I'm significant only when I don't let you decide what I will do."

A child seeking *revenge* has given up on belonging, but believes, "At least I can get even with you for how much you have hurt me, and I know it upsets you if I don't do my homework."

The sad thing about revenge is that children usually choose behavior that hurts them at least as much as the adults with whom they are trying to get even.

A child whose goal is *giving up* believes, "I can't be significant no matter what I do. I give up. Leave me alone."

Imagine that you are a child with each of these beliefs—try to get into the child's world—and imagine how being locked up, confined or isolated would affect you. Then imagine how time out designed to help you feel

27

better would affect you.

A child in the mistaken goal of power could easily perceive time out as an invitation to a power struggle. When a parent insists on winning ("You *will* go to your room and stay there!"), the child feels defeat looming and may escalate the power struggle or switch to revengeful behavior. This is another reason why it is essential to remind children that they have the choice to decide when they feel good enough to behave in ways that are helpful to themselves and others. The escalation of power and revenge can be eliminated when young people understand, in advance, that the purpose of time out is not to punish them, but to help them feel better.

Children pursuing the goal of revenge may have a difficult time believing time out is to help them, not hurt them. It is essential that parents and teachers set up the criteria for positive time out in advance. Time out should never be used for a child stuck in the goal of giving up. This child is usually too discouraged to act out, but may choose time out as a way to avoid experiences that make him feel inadequate. Children who feel this way can best be helped with lots of encouragement and goal disclosure, as explained later.

One way to enforce time out with kindness is to remind children in a loving tone of voice, "Remember, the purpose of time out is not to hurt you, but to give you time to cool off and feel better. You can decide when you feel good enough to join us."

Understanding Perceptions

Even a cursory understanding of the four mistaken goals gives us an idea of how important it is to *get into the child's world* to understand his or her perceptions. The same behavior—for example, arguing—could happen for at least four different reasons:

"I want attention."

"I want power."

"I want to hurt you by making your life difficult."

"I give up feeling capable and can avoid trying by arguing."

Children Do Better When They Feel Better

Whatever the reason for arguing, children need to feel better before they will do better.

29

Positive time out can help children feel better so they will feel like behaving better. If children change their behavior after a few minutes in time out, nothing more is needed! There is no need for further consequences or lectures.

If a parent or teacher begins to notice a *pattern* of misbehavior, a problem-solving session might be appropriate to figure out a solution. In this case, time out might be necessary for a cooling-off period before the child feels good enough to work out a plan of action.

Sometimes adults also need a cooling-off period to feel good enough to deal lovingly and rationally with a problem. It is all but impossible to respond calmly and helpfully when we're angry or upset. Taking time out for ourselves can help us to calm down, to not say or do hurtful things, and to focus on solutions rather than blame.

Are We Looking for Blame or Are We Looking for Solutions?

It's amazing how often parents and teachers have to admit, when they're pushed, that they often focus more on making children *pay* for what they have done than on helping children change to a more useful behavior. Time out as punishment makes them pay—and often encourages resentment and anger—rather than focusing on a plan to improve behavior.

It is tempting to want to be in control, and sentencing children to "15 minutes of time out in your room, young lady!" can feel pretty satisfying to an angry, irritated parent. But if what we want is to encourage positive, long-range results in our children, we will help them assume control over themselves. Time out as a positive experience encourages children to assume control and responsibility for their own behavior.

Will Kids Misuse Time Out?

Adults occasionally object that kids will want to go to positive time out to avoid what they are supposed to be doing. Parents and teachers sometimes worry that time out may seem like a reward for bad behavior.

When children are involved in creating the guidelines for time out and have a clear understanding that the purpose is to help, not punish, they seldom misuse time out as an opportunity to miss being on task. The few cases where this might happen provide an excellent opportunity to diagnose a deeper prob-

31

lem—such as the fourth mistaken goal of be-havior, giving up. Children who sincerely believe they can't do what is expected might choose positive time out as a way to avoid the problem. These children need help, not time out.

Shaun was such a child. Mrs. Williams, his third-grade teacher, noticed Shaun spend-ing extended periods of time in the time-out area hugging a teddy bear. She asked Shaun to come see her after school and followed the process of goal disclosure.

Goal Disclosure

Goal disclosure is an excellent way to di-agnose a child's mistaken goal, but to be ef-fective you must show a friendly attitude and genuinely want to know what the child be-lieves.

The process of goal disclosure includes the following three steps:

1. Ask the child "why" he or she is do-ing a certain behavior (knowing the answer will most likely be, "I don't know").

2. Ask permission to guess why. Most children will give you permission if you have shown them you are friendly and really care

about how they feel. You probably suspect the goal before using goal disclosure, but simply need verification from the child (because parents and teachers can—occasionally—be wrong).

3. Ask, "Could it be _____?" regarding each mistaken goal, as demonstrated in the following example.

When Shaun came in after school, Mrs. Williams set up a friendly atmosphere by first asking him if he had noticed the fascinating cloud formations. Each tried to pick out patterns. Mrs. Williams showed Shaun a rabbit; Shaun pointed out a kite.

Then Mrs. Williams said, "Shaun, I have noticed that you have been going into time out a lot. Do you know why you are using time out so much?"

Shaun said, "I need a cooling-off time to help me feel better." (Kids usually say, "I don't know," but not always.)

Mrs. Williams said, "That may be the reason, but I have another idea. I don't know for sure, but would it be okay with you if I make a couple of guesses?" (It's important to say you don't know, but want to guess—because that's the truth.)

Shaun looked uncertain, but said, "I guess so."

Mrs. Williams asked, "Could it be that using time out is a good way to get my attention and keep me busy with you?"

With a straight face, Shaun said, "No." (It is important to look for a recognition reflex with the answer. If Shaun had said "no" with a grin on his face, he might actually have been saying, "yes." When you get a recognition reflex you acknowledge it by saying something like, "Shaun, your voice says no, but your smile is telling me that could be the reason.")

Mrs. Williams said, "May I guess again?"

Shaun was intrigued; he agreed.

"Could it be that using time out is a good way to show that you are in charge and can do what you want?"

Again Shaun said "no" with no recognition reflex.

Mrs. Williams asked, "Could it be that the reason you use time out a lot is that you feel hurt and want to hurt others by withdrawing from us?"

Shaun said, "No."

Mrs. Williams said, "May I guess one more time?"

Shaun agreed again.

"Could it be that you feel you can't do your work and just want to give up?"

34

Shaun got a tear in his eye and whispered, "I can't."

Mrs. Williams said, "Shaun, I'm so glad to know that's what you think. I can help you with that. Let's work on a plan together."

No matter what the goal, you can work on a plan with the child to solve the problem. For attention, you can work out useful ways to get attention—and you can make a point of giving attention periodically for no reason at all except to show you care. For power, you can find constructive ways for the child to be powerful. For revenge, you can talk about hurt feelings. Talking is often enough to straighten out the cause of the hurt.

Since Shaun's goal was giving up, Mrs. Williams spent extra time for tutoring until she was sure he understood the work and could achieve success. "It didn't really take much extra time," she explained later. "I would just be encouraging for an extra minute or two—that can seem like an eternity to a child who wants to give up. (A child into the mistaken goal of giving up does not enjoy extra time the way a child into the mistaken goal of attention does. Often that's one clue to help you figure out the mistaken goal.) At first Shaun insisted he couldn't do it. Then it seemed as if he did it just to get me off his back. I remember the surprised, pleased look on his face the first time he *didn't* give up and successfully completed his work."

Part of the plan Mrs. Williams worked out with Shaun was for him to choose a classmate to work with until he felt confident to work on his own. Shaun also agreed to tutor a first grader who needed help at a level where Shaun felt confidence. Shaun's sense of belonging and significance improved when he learned both to give and to receive help.

Goal disclosure can help children become consciously aware of their mistaken goals. Awareness increases responsibility, choice and possible change. The Mistaken Goal chart offers several suggestions other than time out for behavior based on any of the four mistaken goals.

Teaching the Mistaken Goals of Misbehavior to Kids

Many parents and teachers talk openly with their children and students about the mistaken goals of misbehavior, and let them know there is a useful side to attention and power, as well as a useless side. One activity that gets children involved to increase their awareness is inviting them to brainstorm on helpful ways to gain attention and to use power.

Mr. Gilbert is a teacher of children labeled with *attention deficit disorder*. His students have learned about the four mistaken goals of misbehavior. They have agreed to help each other with friendly reminders when they notice anyone using these goals in ways that are hurtful to themselves and others. They all have signs for each goal on the end of popsicle sticks. When they notice someone using their power destructively or trying to get attention in useless ways, they hold up their signs. They all understand that the purpose is not to label or stereotype, but rather to be a friendly reminder for the person to drop the useless behavior.

Can you guess who gets the most reminders about power? Yes, Mr. Gilbert, who always says, "Thanks for the reminder. I can see I'm forgetting to get you more involved. Who has some constructive suggestions that would work better?"

Mr. Gilbert shared enthusiastically, "Misbehavior has decreased significantly in my class. The more I get students involved in understanding themselves and each other, and in helping each other in respectful ways, the more belonging and significance they feel. It is true. When kids feel belonging and significance, they don't feel the need to misbehave. I'm not going to say we are all perfect yet, and I do mean 'we.' But we now have a different attitude about the mistakes we make and we know we can help each other grow and improve. The kids get a kick out of helping me improve. It was a big step for me to welcome their help instead of feeling threatened by it. What a relief to let that one go! Teaching is a lot more fun now. And yes, my students are learning more. The better they feel, the better they behave—and the better they feel, the more they learn."

The same principle works for parents. Margaret and her nine-year-old son Rod were having an argument. Rod's parents had divorced recently, and mother and son were both still adjusting to their new lifestyle.

"Time to clean up your room and get ready for bed, Rod—school tomorrow," Margaret announced.

"But Mom, I'm still working on this model," Rod answered. "Can I stay up just a little while longer?"

Margaret had had a long day; work had been stressful, the bills seemed to be piling up faster than she could pay them, and the sink was full of dishes. She answered with more irritation in her voice than she intended, "No, young man—I said now, and I meant *now.*"

Rod's frustration equaled his mother's, and his reply was meant to sting. "You're *always* grumpy these days," he shot back. "I'd rather go live with my dad. He never tells me what to do, and we have fun together. I know why he divorced you; who'd want to live with a grump?"

The door closed with a loud thump, and Margaret could hear Rod angrily putting away his things. She resisted the impulse to burst through the door and respond to her son's painful—and unfair—accusations, knowing that she needed time to cool off, and that behind his closed door Rod was doing some thinking of his own.

After a short while, Margaret heard the door open, and a quiet voice said, "Mom?"

Margaret and her son sat down and talked about what had happened and why, about revenge and why we sometimes strike back to hurt even people we love. They talked about their situation, and how they both needed time to adjust. And Margaret explained that the anger in her voice had more to do with work and stress than it did with Rod, while Rod apologized for having said things he knew would cause his mother pain. Both agreed that they needed time to cool off and to think before they spoke.

Both Mr. Gilbert and Margaret had the courage to live the principle that mistakes truly *are* opportunities to learn, and that help from each other is something to welcome rather than avoid. They also realized and taught that there are times when we might be too upset to welcome help. At those times it helps to take time out until we have calmed down and feel better. Mr. Gilbert and his students, and Margaret and her son, have learned that time out is not the final solution but a time to think, to feel better, and to get ready for productive solutions.

MISTAKEN GOAL CHART

If the PARENT/ TEACHER feels:	And tends to REACT by:	And if the CHILD'S RESPONSE is:	The CHILD'S GOAL is:	The BELIEF behind the CHILD'S BEHAVIOR is:	PARENT/TEACHER ALTERNATIVES include:
Annoyed Irritated Worried Guilty	Reminding. Coaxing. Doing things for the child he/she could do for him/ herself.	Stops temporarily, but later resumes same or another disturbing behavior.	Undue Attention (to keep others busy or to get special service)	I count (belong) only when I'm being noticed or getting special service. I'm only important when I'm keeping you busy with me.	"I love you and ___." (Example: I care about you and will spend time with you later.) Give positive attention at other times. Avoid special service. Say it only once, then act. Plan special time. Set up routines. Take time for training. Use natural and logical consequences. Encourage. Redirect. Use family/class meetings. Touch without words. Ignore. Set up nonverbal signals.
Angry Provoked Challenged Threatened Defeated	Fighting. Increasing control ("I'll make you"). Wanting to be right.	Intensifies behavior. Defiant compliance. Feels he/she's won when parents/ teachers are upset. Passive power.	Power (to be boss)	I belong only when I'm boss or in control, or proving no one can boss me. "You can't make me."	Ask for help. Don't fight and don't give in. Withdraw from conflict. Do the unexpected. Be firm and kind. Act, don't talk. Decide what you will do. Let routines be the boss. Leave and calm down. Develop mutual respect. Give limited choices. Set reasonable and few limits. Practice follow through. Encourage. Use family/class meetings.
Hurt Disappointed Disbelieving Disgusted	Retaliating. Getting even. Thinking: "How could you do this to me?"	Retaliates. Intensifies. Escalates the behavior or chooses another weapon.	Revenge (to get even)	I don't think I belong so I'll hurt others as I feel hurt. I can't be liked or loved.	Deal with the hurt feelings. Avoid punishment and retaliation. Build trust. Use reflective listening. Share your feelings. Make amends. Show you care. Act, don't talk. Encouragement of strengths. Put kids in same boat. Use family/class meetings.
Despair Hopeless Helpless	Giving up. Doing for. Overhelping.	Retreats further. Passive. No improvement. No response.	Assumed Disability (to give up & be left alone)	I can't belong because I'm not perfect, so I'll convince others not to expect anything of me. It's no use trying because I won't do it right.	Show faith. Take small steps. Stop all criticism. Encourage any positive attempt, no matter how small. Focus on assets. Don't pity. Don't give up. Set up opportunities for success. Teach skills/show how. Step back. Enjoy the child. Build on his/her interests. Encourage, encourage, encourage. Use family/class meetings.

Chapter 4

Reward and Punishment

Some parents believe sending children to time out with instructions to do something to help themselves feel better is rewarding their misbehavior. These parents believe children need to suffer and feel bad before they will change their behavior. These are often the same parents who believe that the only way to raise responsible children is by exerting control over them.

Parents and teachers who believe in the necessity of control frequently were raised by authoritarian, controlling parents. And control does "work," at least when children are young enough—and small enough—to be physically moved and controlled.

There is, however, a time bomb built into raising our children with control (and the punishment that frequently accompanies it)—they grow up. And what happens when children become adolescents, too large and too strong-willed to be easily controlled?

Children need discipline; that is not the issue. The problem with the philosophy behind control and punishment, however, is that it makes parents and teachers responsible for children's behavior. How do we raise children who are responsible for their *own* behavior?

Punishment Does Not Produce Positive Long-Range Results

Jane Nelsen shares the following account of her experience on the Oprah Winfrey Show:

I was invited to be on the show to discuss the age-old controversy over spanking. The guests included two parents who believed in spanking and two who did not. Of course, I appreciated the parents who didn't spank and thought they were doing an excellent job. To my horror, they were labeled "permissive parents" on the television monitor. They were not at all permissive. They believed in positive discipline. These positive parents used a time-out chair with their three-year-old called "the happy chair." When their child misbehaved they often asked him to sit in the happy chair until he felt better.

The father who believed in spanking made fun of this idea. He said (I will paraphrase): "Suppose both our kids go to a store and are tempted to steal something. My son will think, 'I'd better not or my parents will kill me.' Your son will think, 'If I do, my parents might make me sit in the happy chair'."

Everyone laughed because it sounded ludicrous that the threat of a happy chair would eliminate the temptation to steal.

I wanted to say to that father (but did not get the chance on the show), "Your child may not steal because he is afraid you might kill him. What will he do when you are not around to make such threats? He will not learn self-discipline and motivation when driven only by your threats."

Another time Jane was on a radio show in Phoenix, Arizona, where she explained the philosophy of sending kids to their rooms to cool off and feel better instead of as a punishment to make them feel bad. She suggested that parents explain to their children that whenever they are in such a bad mood that they need time out, they can go to their room and read a book, play with their toys, listen to music or just rest awhile. When they feel better, they can come out and work on a solution or simply change their behavior.

Jane was driving down the street listening to the radio after the show and heard the host making fun of her philosophy. "Can you imagine," he asked, "rewarding misbehavior by telling your kids to go to their room and do something to make themselves feel better?"

He and many others are convinced that kids have to suffer to learn. He could not hear the part that goes beyond just feeling good to *coming out of the room when ready to work on solutions or to change behavior.*

Eliminate Punishment and Reward

It is a difficult task to convince adults that punishment and reward have no place in the philosophy of positive time out. Punishment and reward teach adults—not kids—to be responsible. When punishment and reward are used, it is the adult's job to *catch* kids when they are *good* and be ready with a reward; and then *catch* kids when they are *bad* and be ready with a punishment. What happens when the adult is not around?

Eliminating punishment and reward is essential for time out to be positive and helpful to kids. It is also the most difficult concept for adults to integrate. Eliminating the word "punishment" from our vocabulary may be the first step in eliminating the belief that punishment is a good motivator for improved behavior.

Punishment and Discipline are not the Same

Adults often react to the suggestion that they eliminate punishment by saying, "Are you kidding? Are you suggesting I let kids do whatever they want?" And the answer is "absolutely not—kids *need* discipline." What they do *not* need is punishment. The word "discipline" comes from the same Greek root as the word "disciple" and means "to teach." The

47

purpose of positive time out—and positive discipline itself—is to help kids learn self-discipline, self-confidence, self-control. Positive time out is just one way to help children improve their behavior by empowering them to make changes.

Chapter 5

Logical Consequences

All human beings (and children *are* human beings) have rights to be treated with dignity and respect, even when they need to experience the consequences of their choices. Most of us will admit that our mistakes and wrong choices are often what teach us the greatest lessons. The concept of logical consequences as a form of discipline enables children to learn from their mistakes and wrong choices in a protected, encouraging environment.

Many people misunderstand the concept of logical consequences as a form of discipline. Logical consequences can become just another punishment when dignity and respect are lacking, or when adults believe children must *feel* bad before they will *do* better.

Punishment often includes humiliating lectures and put downs. Logical consequences require enforcement with dignity and respect. Time out can be a logical consequence when it is used under these conditions, and with the following philosophy.

Kind and Firm at the Same Time

Strange as it seems, we can be kind and firm at the same time when enforcing consequences, rather than humiliating and firm, or angry and firm. A kind and firm parent or teacher says, "I can see you are too upset to behave respectfully. I'm sure time out will help you feel better. You can decide when you're ready to work this out."

An angry, humiliating parent or teacher would say, "You're in time out for half an hour! You'll need to write 50 sentences about your bad behavior."

One of the keys to effective and positive use of logical consequences is that a parent or teacher must use a kind, firm voice to follow through. In most cases it is important that both adult and child understand the consequence of a behavior *before* it occurs. An arbitrary reac-

50

tion to misbehavior that a parent does *to* a child is a punishment, no matter what we call it.

The "Three Rs of Logical Consequences"

The "Three Rs of Logical Consequences" will help parents and teachers to use logical consequences in an appropriate and positive manner. The Three Rs are:

1. **Related**. A consequence must be logically, obviously related to the behavior.

2. **Respectful**. The consequence must be enforced respectfully, without anger, force, or humiliation.

3. **Reasonable**. The consequence must seem reasonable to the child and to the adult.

Logical consequences are often misused and turned into punishment when any one of the Three Rs are not followed. Time out is not related, respectful or reasonable when it is used as a punishment.

Related

Time out is *related* only when children understand how negative feelings affect behavior and that time out can allow a cooling-off period to help them feel better so they can behave better.

Time out is not related when a child perceives that she has been "sentenced" to time out as an arbitrary punishment for misbehavior.

Respectful

Time out is *respectful* only when children know the purpose is to help, not punish. It is respectful when the feeling behind the enforcement is one of dignity and respect. Maintaining dignity and respect at all times can be difficult; but it is essential and can be accomplished only when the adult involved has a tone of voice and attitude that conveys his belief that time out is an opportunity to feel better and work toward solving a problem.

Reasonable

Time out is *reasonable* only when it has been explained to children in advance that it is not for the purpose of humiliation and punishment. It is reasonable—and empowering—when children decide when they are ready to leave time out and be helpful to themselves and others.

Another important factor to ensure that time out is reasonable is to help children see the value for themselves. Children will see the value of time out when they are involved in the advance planning for the use of time out and can help design ways they will use it to help themselves feel better (as discussed in Chapter 6).

Children can understand the value of time out when we explain how this consequence is related to behavior. A teacher might say, "When you don't treat your friends kindly or follow the playground rules, the logical consequence is to lose the privilege of using the playground until you are ready to treat people and things with respect."

The Feeling Behind What You Do is More Important Than What You Do

It's been said many times before and will undoubtedly be said many times in the future: the feeling behind what we do makes all the difference as to whether time out is a punishment or a consequence, whether it is encouraging or discouraging, whether it is effective or ineffective for children in the long run.

One mother reported that time out "never works for me." She had been confining her strong-willed toddler to a "time out chair," with an egg timer ticking away one minute for each year of his age. Her son, outraged at his confinement, resorted to tossing everything within reach at his frazzled mother and struggling relentlessly to get free.

This mother noticed an obvious improvement when she enforced time out with dignity and respect: "I see you're not feeling good enough to be respectful to me right now. You may have a time out in your room until you feel better, and you can come out as soon as you're ready to do better." The power struggle ended because Mom was no longer hooked into it, and time out became an effective way for both mother and son to feel better.

One school district found that the main reason it had such a negative school climate was because the staff was enforcing logical consequences with humiliation and put downs: "You sit on the time-out bench and think about how disrespectful you've been. You've lost the privilege of using the playground for two days."

54

The staff reported that the school climate changed when they enforced logical consequences with dignity and respect: "I'm sorry you're not feeling good enough to be respectful to yourself and others. You may sit on the feel good bench until you feel better. Join us as soon as you know you're ready."

Another Misuse of Logical Consequences

Turning logical consequences into punishment is only one danger. Another lies in thinking that logical consequences should be applied to every misbehavior (or believing that time out is a logical consequence for every misbehavior).

If you look at the Goal Chart on page 41, you will notice a number of possible responses to mistaken goal behavior. Other suggestions are explained in detail in the Positive Discipline and Developing Capable People materials (see the Annotated Bibliography on page 99).

The need for time out may never be eliminated. Who doesn't need a quiet place to calm down, cool off and feel better once in a while?

Wouldn't it be nice if adults used positive time out for themselves more often?

The need for time out can be reduced—in fact, the need to misbehave can be reduced—when children feel a sense of belonging, significance, and capability. Perhaps the most effective parenting tool is a preventative one: encouraging children, noticing their good behavior and contributions to the family and classroom, getting them involved in family and class meetings, and empowering them to solve their own problems.

Chapter 6

Encouragement

A misbehaving child is usually a discouraged child. And it follows that one way to eliminate misbehavior is by encouraging children, helping them to feel that they have significance, belonging, and an appropriate sort of power over their lives and choices.

Getting Children Involved in Planning for Time Out

Parents and teachers can involve young people in creating the guidelines for positive time out. Children are usually more willing to follow rules they've had a voice in making, and answering questions like these can give them a sense of involvement and empowerment— as well as making time out more likely to accomplish its purpose;

1. Why or how does a cooling-off period help people?

2. What can we do to make sure time out is helpful and not humiliating?

3. What can we do to make sure time out is related, respectful and reasonable?

4. Where should the time out area be, and what are some things you could do in time out to help you feel better?

One school class decided they would have teddy bears and pillows in the time-out area. They also decided that each child would take responsibility for deciding when he or she felt better and was ready to rejoin the class. A kitchen timer was provided for those who wanted to make a guess about how much time they would need.

Another class decided they would have notebooks in the time-out area so they could write about their feelings if they felt like it. The teacher of this class had taught the journaling process and these children had learned that writing journal style gave them perspective they didn't have before writing.

One youngster kept a cozy corner of her room stocked with favorite books, stuffed animals, and a tape recorder with music. Going to the time out corner was an opportunity for her to have a few moments with things she knew would help her to feel better—and she sometimes chose to stay there quite contentedly!

When time out helps children understand that we can all feel discouraged at times and that they can decide when they are ready to change their behavior, they will feel encouraged—the basis of belonging and significance.

Positive Time Out is Not a Reward

Parents and teachers occasionally worry that children will misbehave on purpose so they can spend time out in such a pleasant place, but this rarely happens when the guidelines discussed so far have been followed. If a child is using time out as a way of avoiding work or relationships, parents may need to spend some time with the child to find out whether there is a deeper problem, and how they can work to encourage that child and build his sense of belonging and significance.

Age-Appropriate Strategies

"Oh terrific," you may be saying. "I know some teenagers who would take this 'feel good' idea and run with it!" One high school teacher expressed concern about allowing high school students to create a time-out area that would make them feel good. He could just see the wild posters, hear the loud music, and smell the cigarette smoke. And he was sure that most teens would go out of their way to have time out in such a rad place.

He is right. The developmental stage of adolescents (individuation and testing their personal power) is one reason a really cool time-out area might not be a good idea. Another excellent approach for dealing with adolescents' discipline issues is described in Chapter 7. However, some high school teachers have found positive time out to be successful with their students. The key to success was that these teachers provided a learning environment where students wanted to be, and the students were involved in planning the time out. They discussed the issue of students taking advantage and decided that people who abused the opportunity would lose it.

Using Influence or Losing Influence

When adults help children feel better (encouraged), they create closeness and trust. And when children can trust the adults in their lives, they have less incentive to misbehave—and more opportunity to learn the positive, long-term skills of responsibility and self-discipline. Upon a foundation of closeness and trust, adults have influence to help children develop the skills they need to control their behavior.

When adults insist on remaining in full control, and when they resort to punishment and humiliation, they create resistance and hostility in their children and they lose the opportunity for trust and positive influence.

John Taylor's Thermometer

In his book *Person to Person*, John Taylor describes a role-play activity that helps adults understand a child's perceptions and experience the difference between closeness and trust and distance and hostility.

Two volunteers play a child and an adult who start out facing each other about four feet apart. The "child" is given the following instructions: "Whenever the 'adult' says something that makes you feel encouraged, move toward him. Whenever the adult says something that makes you feel discouraged move further away. Do not respond verbally." The adult is then instructed, "Start out by making punitive statements intended to make the child feel guilty or bad. Then change your tactics and make positive statements to help the child feel understood and encouraged."

Here is one example of what happened when two people tried this activity:

Adult: I heard you were misbehaving on the playground again! When are you going to learn to be more respectful? (Child moves away.)

Adult: Well, don't you have anything to say for yourself? (Child moves further away.)

Adult: Well, you can just sit on the time-out bench for a week and see if that will teach you! (Child moves further away.)

Adult, now using a friendly voice: I heard there was a problem on the playground, and I would really like to hear your side of the story. (Child moves closer.)

Adult: I can understand why you feel upset; sometimes I feel the same way. (Child moves closer.)

Adult: Would you be willing to do something to help you feel better until you can work on a solution? (Child moves closer.)

Adult: Why don't you decide how much time you need on the feel good bench, and well give the other child the same opportunity. (Child moves closer.)

Things Often Get Worse Before They Get Better

We live in a "fast-food" society; sometimes we expect that when we make changes, we will see instant results. We have been programmed to think of time out as a punishment for misbehavior rather than an encouraging way to solve a problem, and it can take time for old attitudes to change—both for us and for our children!

It will take time for both adults and children to absorb the idea that time out can be a positive, encouraging experience rather than just another form of punishment, and it may be helpful to occasionally remind children that we don't want them to feel bad—we want them to feel better!

It is well worth the effort and time it takes (usually three to six weeks) for children—and adults—to get used to *positive* time out.

Change won't happen overnight; but anything that not only helps a child improve behavior, but encourages and builds a sense of belonging, significance, self-control, and self-discipline is worth the time and effort it takes.

Chapter 7

Ask What?

There is a simple key to getting into a child's world and learning how he thinks and feels. Don't *tell* what: *ask* "what?" Well-meaning adults often tell kids what happened, how they should feel about what happened, and what they should do next time; after all, we reason, we've been around a lot longer and we've learned a few things. We say well-meaning because we know adults believe this is a good way to teach children.

Unfortunately, it's not. Children don't learn when we stuff information in. Children learn when we draw information out and help them put the pieces of the puzzle together for themselves, to ask questions and to learn from their own answers. The word "education" is derived from the Latin root *educare*—which means "to draw forth."

We draw forth and help children learn when we ask them, "What happened? What do you think caused it to happen? How do you feel about what happened? What did you learn? What could you do differently next time if you wanted to prevent it from happening again?"

"Ask what?" is a shorthand version of the EIAG process that helps children develop perceptions, wisdom and judgment from their life experiences. The following explanation of the EIAG process is quoted from the book *Raising Self-Reliant Children in a Self-Indulgent World*:

1. **Experience**: Become aware of experiences, both negative and positive, in your child's life.

2. **Identify**: Help your child identify the significant elements or outcome of a particular event. "What happened? What did you see? What are you feeling? What was the most important thing?"

3. **Analyze**: Help your child analyze why aspects of the event were important. "Why was that significant to you? Why do you think it happened?" Sometimes, though, the question "why" can sound like an attack; after all, parents and teachers often say things like "Why

did you do that?" or "Why didn't you do as I said?" It may be less threatening to say, "What made that seem important to you? What were you trying to do? What caused you to feel that way?"

4. **Generalize**: Help your child distill from the experience a single principle that can be remembered and used in a similar situation. "How can you use this information in the future? How can you do it differently next time for different results? What do you need to do if you want the same results again?"

One of the most common errors in working with young people is to assume that they understand and interpret what they experience as a mature person would. By using the four steps of the EIAG process this way, we clarify, affirm and validate the perceptions of the young person we are working with.

Applying the EIAG process—whether in the classroom, at home, in counseling or in other personal relationships—helps us avoid preaching and lecturing, and enables us to help young people personalize their life experiences and develop their perceptions.

How does this apply to time out? Negative—punitive—time out does not help children use their judgment and wisdom to analyze

67

what happened, what caused it to happen or what they could do differently.

Kent Mann, principal at Lexington High School in Lexington, Nebraska, developed a system for working with students sent to his office (an interesting form of time out) for behavior problems. According to Mann, this system has reduced hostility between students, teachers and administrators and given students an opportunity to express their perceptions and help resolve the disciplinary problems.

The Resolution Process: Stage I

When students are sent to the principal's office as a discipline referral from the classroom, they receive a Student Incident Report on which they are asked to respond in writing to these questions:

1. Please give a brief summary of what happened in the classroom. (Experience)

2. Identify the key issues (people or circumstances) related to the incident. (Identify)

3. What occurred that actually caused the problem? (Analyze)

4. How would you suggest that a situation like this be handled in the future so that problems might be avoided? (Generalize)

68

The students write this report privately in a work area in the office. This period of time frequently allows them an opportunity to regain their composure and also serves as an appropriate *cool-down* period before they discuss the problem.

The Resolution Process: Stage II

As soon as a student has completed the Student Incident Form, a conference with the principal is held. During the conference, the EIAG process is again implemented. The conference opens with these three questions?

1. How are you feeling?
2. What exactly is the problem?
3. What are you willing to do about it?

After discussing these questions, the information provided on the Student Incident Form is reviewed by the student and the principal. Clarifications are made and details are added as needed. If a series of referrals has occurred, the principal may review prior incident reports with the student and attempt to identify a common pattern of behavior or a recurring problem.

Accountability is also discussed during the conference. The student is asked if, in his or her opinion, the situation that has occurred merits some type of consequence. If the student's response is in favor of some type of consequence, he or she is asked to recommend a type of consequence. In most instances, a consensus agreement is reached between the student and the principal related to the need for and type of consequence. The conference is concluded when the problem has been resolved with a solution that is both realistic and fair. However, Stage III activities may be initiated by either the student or the principal.

The Resolution Process: Stage III (optional)

A series of follow-up conference opportunities are available and included on the Student Incident Form. The intent of these options is to assist the student in making a smooth transition back to the classroom setting by building a support system and communicating information to other involved parties about the problem incident. Options for possible implementation include:

1. Making an appointment with the teacher to allow the student to share a plan of

future action and discuss the student's return to class.

2. Making an appointment with the school counselor.

3. Scheduling a student-teacher-principal meeting.

4. Arranging for a parent/guardian conference.

5. Other requests initiated by the student or principal.

This application of the EIAG process has yielded positive results in working with high school disciplinary problems. Documentation of the student's feelings can be used to better understand the individual and some of his or her personal needs and feelings.

In addition, students are far more likely to respond positively to consequences and boundaries when they have had some input, and when they have been treated with dignity and respect.

Finally, the dialogue between student and principal allows the principal to participate with the student in finding a solution to the problem, and builds a positive and productive relationship. This procedure gets past hostility and anger and helps students change their behavior while maintaining dignity and respect.

71

EIAG At Home

It's not hard to see that with a little modification, this process works well at home too. Jim has promised his 16-year-old son Ryan that he may use the family car to take a friend to the movies, as long as the lawn is mowed first. Ryan knows the conditions and has agreed to mow the lawn, but—well, there was a great football game on, and then a friend or two called on the phone, and time just slipped away. Now Ryan has the car keys in his hand, it's time to leave, and the lawn isn't mowed—and Jim has to follow through.

Kindly but firmly he informs Ryan that because their agreement hasn't been met he will not be able to use the car. In his frustration Ryan throws down the keys, shouts at his father, and slams the door to his room behind him.

Jim is sorely tempted to follow his son and tell him how he feels about his behavior. But Jim realizes that time alone will help Ryan calm down, and when he does he may remember their agreement and be more willing to talk constructively about it.

Just before dinner a rather sheepish Ryan appears in the den. "How are you feeling,

Ryan?" Jim asks quietly. Ryan is still unhappy, but as Jim leads him through the EIAG process, he is able to accept responsibility for his own decision not to mow the lawn as he'd promised, and to realize that next time, football games and phone calls notwithstanding, he'll keep his end of the bargain if he wants to use the car. Jim has been saved the hassle of losing his temper and lecturing, and Ryan is more likely to learn from his experience.

The Two P's of Empowerment

Barbara Coloroso, author and lecturer of the "Kids Are Worth It" and "Winning at Teaching and Parenting" series, shares our views on creating a positive home and classroom environment. She emphasizes the importance of teaching children *how* to think, not *what* to think. An important part of this process is what Barbara calls "The Two P's of Empowerment". They are:

1. Ownership of the Problem; and
2. Responsibility for the Plan.

We often usurp opportunities for children to feel empowered by telling them our judgment of what the problem is, as well as telling them what they should do about it. We can actually help our children learn more quickly by guiding them in developing and learning from their own perceptions.

Punishment does not empower. Punishment teaches the attitudes and skills of shame and avoidance rather than ownership and responsibility. Positive time out, as well as the EIAG process, gives young people an opportunity to learn and practice the "Two P's of Empowerment" when they see the value of a cooling-off period and time to work on a plan.

Chapter 8

Going Beyond Time Out

Learning is a lifelong process, and neither children nor adults are likely to outgrow the need for occasional time outs to cool off until they can behave appropriately. However, time out should never be considered the "end of the story." The story continues when we teach children vital life skills such as social interest and problem-solving skills.

Social Interest

Alfred Adler believed that mental health, including self-esteem, is directly related to the amount of social interest one has. Social interest means the genuine interest we have in others and in our social community. When we're not feeling healthy or good about who we are, we tend to withdraw from relationships and from our community; this is a lack of social interest, and children as well as adults experience it.

Problem-solving skills help children to be interested in others and to respect differences. Group problem-solving (such as family or class meetings) teaches the importance of social interest and problem-solving skills in the community of family or classroom.

Get Children Involved in Solutions

When kids are involved in solutions to problems they face in their families or classrooms, they have a feeling of ownership and an incentive to follow plans they help create. There are several ways to encourage young people to be involved in problem solving: we can use one-on-one problem solving between teacher and student, parent and child, or two children, or we can organize and have regular family/class meetings.

One-on-One Problem Solving Between Two Young People

Jane shares what she learned as an elementary school counselor about getting students involved in solutions. (It's fairly easy to see how the same ideas could be applied to siblings or to fights among friends.)

Jane relates: Students would often be sent to my office for fighting. In the beginning, I would make the mistake of trying to help them solve their fights by listening to their stories and coming up with suggestions for solutions. They always argued with my suggestions; they wanted me to take sides. (Remember that rivalry or arguments between kids are often designed to win power or adult attention!)

I decided to leave the counseling office and let them work things out themselves based on one rule: "Forget about blame, and work on solutions." I told them to come out and let me know their plan as soon as they had worked it out. I was amazed at how quickly they could work things out when I would leave them alone with that one rule.

When I stayed in the office we could talk for ten minutes and the kids would seem angrier than ever and not have any solutions. The

77

first time I left two kids alone to work things out, they were finished in about two minutes. One student agreed to give his opponent one of his T-shirts because his had been ripped in the fight. The other student agreed that he would let his opponent get ahead of him in the lunch line for a week because he had crowded in front and started the fight.

Problem Solving Guidelines

The following guidelines for solving problems are taken from *Positive Discipline*. They allow us to work with others to settle disagreements and resolve problems in a healthy, positive way. Parents and teachers should become familiar with the steps, and practice them with young people so they're comfortable *before* conflict arises:

1. Ignore the provocation. (It takes more courage to walk away than to stay and fight.)

    a. Do something else. (Find another game or activity.)

    b. Leave long enough for a cooling-off period, then settle it.

2. Talk it over respectfully.

    a. Tell the other person how you feel. Let him or her know you don't like what is happening.

      b. Listen without interrupting to what the other person has to say about how he or she feels and what he or she doesn't like.

      c. Take turns sharing what each of you thinks you did to contribute to the problem.

      d. Take turns sharing what each of you is willing to do differently.

      e. Brainstorm on other possible solutions.

    3. Choose a solution or solutions you can both agree on from 2d and 2e above.

    4. If you just can't work it out together, ask for help.

      a. Put it on the class/family meeting agenda.

      b. Talk it over with a parent, teacher or friend.

Take Time For Training

Before conflict occurs, it helps to allow time for kids to role play the above problem-solving steps with some hypothetical situations such as conflict over use of playground equipment, shoving in line, name-calling, or fighting over a toy.

Family and Class Meetings

One of the most powerful tools available for solving problems, setting boundaries, and communicating in an encouraging and positive way is the family or class meeting. These meetings provide a format for children to learn and experience problem-solving skills, logical consequences, understanding and respect for differences, and so many other ingredients that lead to a sense of belonging and significance.

Family or class meetings teach kids and adults to help each other with positive solutions, rather than hurt each other with blame and punitive methods. During a successful family or class meeting children experience every one of the *significant seven* perceptions and skills they need to be confident and successful in life. They learn:

1. "I am capable."
2. "I can make a meaningful contribution."
3. "I can influence what happens in my world."
4. "I can use self-discipline and self-control."
5. "I can use good communication skills to work with others."

6. "I am willing to be accountable for the consequences of my choices and to let others help me work on solutions to learn from my mistakes."

7. "I can use my wisdom and judgment to handle any challenge that comes my way."

We could all use a good, healthy dose of these perceptions and skills!

You may be shaking your head by now and sighing, "This all sounds like an awful lot of work." There is no question that it is much easier for adults simply to tell kids how to solve problems, rather than taking the time to allow them to develop and hone their own problem-solving skills. After all, they will make mistakes and errors of judgment, and we know so much better.

Still, when adults take the easy way out, going for short-range solutions rather than long-range teaching, they rob children of the opportunity to learn the skills they so desperately need to survive and prosper in life.

The importance of family/class meetings cannot be overemphasized. Information on how to implement these meetings is contained in *Positive Discipline*, and readers are urged to explore the concept further there.

Family and class meetings are wonderful

tools to help children and adults improve their behavior and relationships, but they are not magic pills for perfection.

Building the Relationship

Among the greatest keys to building trust, confidence and problem-solving abilities are communication, the art of listening, respect, and love. Since the primary goal of children is to achieve a sense of belonging and significance, what better way to help them feel those things than by spending time listening, understanding, and helping them to feel appreciated and loved?

We live in a busy world, and parents and teachers can easily be overwhelmed by the sheer number of tasks that need to be done. Sometimes our relationships with those we love can be stretched to the breaking point by the rush and stress of daily life, and no single technique of discipline or behavior management will solve our problems.

Sometimes children resort to attention-getting misbehaviors because they have a legitimate *need* for focused attention from the adults in their lives. Shaping behavior and encouraging life skills goes beyond time out, logical consequences or family meetings; it requires time, patience, love and understanding.

It helps to remember that children's needs are much like those of adults. We want to feel that our contributions are noticed, that someone cares about what we've done or how we feel, that someone loves us—and so do our children. It is a powerful thing to take time just to *listen* with undivided attention, to get down on a child's level and make eye contact when we speak, to use friendly touches and hugs as well as words to communicate love and affection.

Janice was in the midst of an important business call when her six-year-old daughter Meg came home from school. It had been a hectic day; Janice was behind in her work, the house was a mess, and laundry was spilling out of the hamper. She still had to arrange for child care in order to attend a meeting that evening, and her nerves were close to fraying.

Meg, on the other hand, had had a wonderful day at school and wanted to share it with her mother, who had seemed more distracted and tense than usual lately. There hadn't been much time for reading, for story telling, or for simply being together. And today she had a

83

really *neat* picture that she had painted all by herself; she couldn't wait to show her mom.

"Mom," she said excitedly, tugging at Janice's sleeve, "Mom, look at my picture."

"Excuse me," Janice said into the receiver; then, to Meg, "Not now, Meg; can't you see I'm on the phone? You know our rules about that."

But Meg couldn't wait. "Mom," she persisted, more loudly this time. "Mom, I want to show you my picture!"

Her mom, completely exasperated now, said, more angrily than she'd intended, "Obviously, Meg, you can't seem to follow our rules. You'd better go to your room for some time out until you feel better!"

Meg, lower lip trembling, disappeared. And Janice, phone call finally ended, collapsed on the couch with a sigh. After a moment of time out for herself, she walked into her daughter's room to find Meg sitting dejectedly on the floor, looking at a book.

Janice gently turned the little girl until she could look directly into her eyes and lovingly stroked her cheek. "You're feeling pretty disappointed, aren't you?" she asked Meg. Meg, lower lip now trembling violently, nodded. "I know I've been too busy lately, and we haven't had much time together. And I've been feeling really stressed, and I know that makes me impatient. Would you forgive me for losing my temper? And would you show me your picture? I really do want to see it, you know."

Meg and Janice sat down together on the bed to examine the picture Meg had painted; afterwards they talked for a while, and then ate a cozy dinner together. While Janice still had to leave for her meeting, she arranged with her daughter for a special time together that weekend, and they shared a big hug.

Time out was a part of what happened; but far more important were the trust and love that built a bridge between mother and daughter.

Sometimes our expectations from ourselves, our family life, and those we love are unrealistically high; we need to realize that children, like adults, will have grumpy days and bad moods, and misbehavior will probably never completely disappear. Still, by working on encouragement and positive ways of relating to our children, including the positive use of time out, we can not only help them control their behavior, but we can give them the self-control and self-esteem to tackle life with confidence.

Chapter 9

Putting It All Together

Tyler was a student in Mr. Lewis's fifth grade class who habitually displayed extremely difficult behavior. He would lose his temper and become violent, hit other kids, knock over desks and tear books.

Mr. Lewis was at his wit's end. He felt he had tried everything: he had sent Tyler to the principal's office; he had made Tyler write 100 sentences stating, "I will not lose my temper in class;" and he had made Tyler stand outside the classroom door for punitive time out.

Since Mr. Lewis's intention was to punish, none of these tactics were effective. Tyler would be fine in the principal's office, but would come back to the classroom and soon lose his temper again. After writing sentences about not losing his temper, he seemed more angry and volatile than ever. When he was standing outside the classroom door, he would distract the other students by making funny faces through the window.

Mr. Lewis decided to try a combination of the suggestions outlined in this book. He started by changing his attitude to one of dignity and respect instead of punishment and shame. He asked Tyler to stay after school one day. With a friendly tone of voice, Mr. Lewis asked Tyler if he had ever noticed what happened in his body when he lost his temper. Tyler belligerently said, "No." (We need to remember that it will take kids awhile to realize and trust that we have changed our attitude. Tyler was used to being punished and shamed, and he had his defenses up.)

Mr. Lewis continued in a calm and friendly manner by sharing about himself. "Tyler, I lose my temper sometimes, and I have noticed that when I am paying attention to my body at those times I can feel tension and stiffness in my neck. In other words, I get a pain in my neck." Mr. Lewis noticed Tyler was paying attention. (Mr. Lewis was admitting that he has the same problem Tyler has—that he sometimes loses his temper. Of course that would interest Tyler.)

Mr. Lewis went on to ask Tyler if he would be willing to do a little experiment and pay attention to his body the next time he lost his temper to see what was happening. Tyler's manner still seemed a bit belligerent and suspicious, but he agreed.

Mr. Lewis shared that Tyler did not lose his temper for five days in a row—a record for Tyler. It is our guess that the special time Mr. Lewis spent with Tyler helped him feel encouraged enough that he could suspend his misbehavior for a while. (One-on-one sharing in a friendly manner can be very powerful and encouraging.) On the sixth day Tyler started fighting with another student. Mr. Lewis put his hand on Tyler's shoulder and whispered in his ear, "Did you notice what happened to your body? Come see me after school and tell me about it." That was enough to diffuse the temper outburst, and Tyler went back to his desk with a thoughtful expression on his face.

After school he explained to Mr. Lewis that he noticed his hands clenched into a fist when he lost his temper and he felt like hitting something. (And, he usually did.) Mr. Lewis asked Tyler, "Would you be willing to use this information to create a plan that can help you control your temper so you will feel better about yourself? We can work on a plan together if you'd like." Tyler agreed.

The plan they agreed on was that whenever Tyler felt his hands clenching into a fist, he would step outside the classroom door and count to ten (or ten thousand), look at the clouds and nature, or whatever it took to help him cool down and feel better. When he was ready he could come back into the classroom. They agreed that he would not need to tell Mr. Lewis when he wanted to stand outside the door because he was working on self-control.

Again, Tyler did not have a temper tantrum for several days. On about the fifth day Mr. Lewis noticed Tyler leave the classroom to stand outside the door. He stood there looking up at the sky. Mr. Lewis said, "I don't know if he was counting or just looking at the clouds, but it was different from when he would spend his time making faces through the window."

In about four minutes Tyler came back into the classroom looking very satisfied with himself. Mr. Lewis went over to him, put his hand on his shoulder and said, "You handled that beautifully, Tyler. Way to go."

Mr. Lewis ended this story by saying, "I'm not going to tell you Tyler never had another temper tantrum in class, because he did; however, he improved significantly. He used to have three or four tantrums a week. Now he has two or three a month. I'll take it!"

Improvement Is A Life-Long Process

We need to remember that perfectionism is extremely discouraging. Adults often seem to expect more from kids than they can accomplish themselves. How many of us are still working on something—like being on time, losing weight, controlling our temper or other areas where we might improve—but never obtain perfection?

Work On Improvement, Not Perfection

Mr. Lewis continued to work with Tyler regularly. When Tyler would lose his temper, Mr. Lewis would see him after school and remind him how much he had improved. Mr.

Lewis even told Tyler that he had been an inspiration to him, "I have controlled my temper better by watching how well you do, but I'm not perfect yet either."

There are many methods—both short-range and long-range—that work to change misbehavior and improve children's self-esteem. Positive time out can help improve behavior without sacrificing self-esteem.

Chapter 10

The Power of Love

You have heard it before, but it always bears repeating: Never underestimate the power of love. What matters most in life to a child is knowing that the important people in her life—parents, teachers, family, friends— love her and believe in her intrinsic worth as a human being. Of course, children aren't consciously aware of this deep need, nor can they always verbalize it; yet they always know somehow when the need to belong and to be loved hasn't been met. This need carries over to school, too: research shows that the main predictor of a child's achievement in school is his or her perception of "Does the teacher *like* me?"

The power of love is beautifully illustrated in the following story by Betsy Licciardello, a teacher of special education in Roseville, California:

I've taught special education for ten years. I heard Jane Nelsen speak four or five years ago and began incorporating her Positive Discipline approach at home and at school.

This year I have a little girl in class who comes from an abusive home. She suffers from severe self-esteem problems. She also wet and soiled her pants daily at school. My aide and I tried many solutions. We cleaned her up—she adored the attention. We had her clean herself up—no improvement. We tried hugs for dry pants every half hour and had very inconsistent results.

One day, as I was walking this girl to the office for dry socks (she had soaked herself all the way to her shoes), I decided to just tell her how I felt about her. I told her, "I love you and will always love you, no matter what you do—good days or bad. I will love you even if you wet your pants every day, or if you never wet your pants again. I like dry pants better, but I will love you no matter what you choose—wet pants or dry."

She hasn't wet her pants at school since we had this little "talk." We have the "talk" every once in a while as a reminder, and we still have lots of hugs. We no longer have wet pants. Hooray!

The most important part of this story is that Betsy really meant it when she said she would love this little girl even if she continued to wet her pants. Betsy didn't just pretend, or use a declaration of love to manipulate change; it's important to realize that children can almost always tell the difference. However, change is often inspired by unconditional love, freely offered. Betsy understands the power of love. May her story be an inspiration to others.

Adults would undoubtedly be much happier if the children in their care never misbehaved or felt the need for time out. But this is the real world and we're all human, adults and children alike; mood swings, bad days, stress, and unforeseen catastrophes are a fact of life for all of us. Consistent use of encouragement and positive, empowering ways of interacting with one another can help children feel sufficient belonging and significance so that they rarely need time out. Teaching children—and adults!—the value of positive time out as an opportunity to catch their breath, calm down and feel better, or to evaluate and learn from their experiences through the EIAG process, is a gift that can serve them throughout their lives.

If we're honest, most of us will admit that we long to feel in control of our lives, and especially of our children. But while locking children in boxes, withdrawing privileges that have nothing to do with the misbehavior, spanking, shaking, and other forms of punishment may give us the illusion of being in control for the moment, the long-range results are never in the best interests of children, or society as a whole.

Ask a group of parents what they really want for their children and they'll usually tell you they want their children to be "happy." Ask them what sort of adults they want those children to become and they have to think a bit harder, but they'll eventually come up with qualities like responsible, independent, wise, confident, compassionate, kind, honest, respectful and industrious.

Those qualities don't just happen; we have to build them into our children from their earliest days and, yes, it takes a lot of hard work. It's worth remembering, too, that parents are only human; we all makes mistakes more often than we would like.

But a relationship that is built on love,

trust, encouragement and hope will endure an amazing number of mistakes. Perhaps we should remember the wisdom offered by Will Rogers when he said, "Quality is a lot like buying oats. If you want fresh, clean, first-quality oats, you have to pay a fair price. If you can be satisfied with oats that have been through the horse, those come quite a bit cheaper."

A relationship with our children that is based on mutual dignity and respect carries a price; but aren't our children worth the effort?

Time Out

ANNOTATED BIBLIOGRAPHY

The following materials are available from Empowering People Books, Tapes & Videos, P.O. Box B, Provo, UT 84603. For a free newsletter and/or to order with a Visa or Mastercard, call toll-free—1-800-456-7770—or use the form on page 111 to place your order.

BOOKS BY JANE NELSEN AND H. STEPHEN GLENN

Positive Discipline by Jane Nelsen is written for parents and teachers. This book includes many examples from homes and classrooms of effective methods for teaching children self-discipline, responsibility, cooperation and problem-solving skills. Chapters 7 and 8 include thorough instructions for implementing class meetings and family meetings. (Ballantine Books, New York, 1987) Price: $9.95. **Order #B101** (Wt. 1 lb.)

Raising Self-Reliant Children In A Self-Indulgent World by H. Stephen Glenn and Jane Nelsen. This book includes information on each of the "Significant Seven" perceptions and skills and other concepts that help children be successful in life. A breakthrough program no parent or teacher can afford to ignore. (Prima Publishing & Communications, Rocklin, CA, 1988) Price: $10.95. **Order #B102** (Wt. 1 lb.)

99

Understanding: Eliminating Stress and Finding Serenity in Life and Relationships by Jane Nelsen explains four principles that can help you experience your inner wisdom, happiness and peace of mind. Many have shared that this book has helped them improve relationships with spouses, children, bosses, colleagues and themselves. (Prima Publishing & Communications, Rocklin, CA, 1988) Price: $9.95. **Order #B103** (Wt. 1 lb.)

Clean and Sober Parenting by Jane Nelsen, Riki Intner and Lynn Lott is a guide to help recovering parents give up guilt and shame, rebuild trust, create structure and routine, and improve communication. Effective parenting skills can break old patterns of co-dependence and enhance the recovery process. Many parents never take the time to learn effective parenting skills. This book gives recovering parents an opportunity to create beauty out of devastation. (Prima Publishing & Communications, Rocklin, CA, 1992) Price: $10.95. **Order #B106** (Wt. 1 lb.) (See page 108 for *Parenting in Recovery: The Next Step Facilitator's Guide*)

Positive Discipline in the Classroom by Jane Nelsen, Lynn Lott and H. Stephen Glenn teaches skills for cooperation, collaboration, communication, problem-solving, mutual respect and much more through the use of class meetings. Class meetings and all positive discipline methods create a classroom climate that enhances academic learning. This book presents the "Eight Building Blocks for Effective Class Meetings" and includes activities and step-by-step methods to teach the building blocks to students. Every teacher wanting to start class meetings should read this book first. (Prima Publishing & Communications, Rocklin, CA, 1993) Price: $14.95. **Order #B107** (Wt. 1 lb.) (See page 108 for *Positive Discipline in the Classroom Facilitator's Guide* which includes classroom and/or inservice activities)

Positive Discipline A-Z by Jane Nelsen, Lynn Lott and H. Stephen Glenn addresses almost every parenting problem you can imagine—in alphabetical order. It offers several short, simple "what to do" solutions. It includes suggestions that help prevent the problem in the future. Children feel good about themselves and gain self-confidence, self-discipline, responsibility, problem-solving skills and healthy self-esteem when parents and teachers use these methods. (Prima Publishing & Communications, Rocklin, CA, 1993) Price: $14.95. **Order #B108** (Wt. 1 lb.)

Positive Discipline for Single Parents by Jane Nelsen, Cheryl Erwin and Carol Delzer teaches positive parenting skills to help parents raise responsible, respectful, resourceful children. It addresses issues of dating, dealing with the other parent, overwhelming time and financial pressures, and much more. In a casual but practical format, this book utilizes everyday examples to help single parents gain confidence, learn problem-solving skills, and turn every member of the family into an active part of the growing-up process. (Prima Publishing & Communications, Rocklin, CA, 1994) Price: $10.95. **Order #B109** (Wt. 1 lb.) (See page 109 for *Facilitator's Guide for Positive Discipline for Single Parents*)

Positive Discipline for Teenagers by Jane Nelsen and Lynn Lott gives parents creative and practical ways to help adolescents take constructive steps toward self-reliance, confidence, courage and life skills. It supports parents in taking kids seriously, listening and communicating well, demonstrating faith that children will use good judgment, holding them accountable, employing logical conse-quences, holding family meetings, using cooperative problem-solving and focusing on issues rather than personalities. Don't wait until your children reach their teens to read this book! (Formerly *I'm On Your Side: Resolving Conflict with Your Teenage Son or Daughter*) (Prima Publishing & Communications, Rocklin, CA, 1990) Price: $14.95. **Order #B110** (Wt. 1 lb.)

Positive Discipline for Preschoolers by Jane Nelsen, Cheryl Erwin and Roslyn Duffy offers practical solutions for every parent and teacher of young children. We hug our little ones, laugh with them, buy them presents, brag about them, and celebrate them. And yet, when it comes time to give them the guidance they need, many of us hesitate. How can I begin to teach boundaries to my six-month-old? Should I spank my two-year-old? What can I do about my defiant four-year-old? Is it all right for my toddler to sleep in my bed? Find the answers to these questions and many more. (Prima Publishing & Communications, Rocklin, CA, 1994) Price: $12.95. **Order #B111** (Wt. 1 lb.) (See page 109 for *Positive Discipline for Preschoolers Facilitator's Guide.*)

AUDIO CASSETTE TAPES BY H. STEPHEN GLENN AND JANE NELSEN

Developing Capable People by H. Stephen Glenn. This six-tape set includes (1) Changing Relationships, (2) Five Keys To Perception, (3) Perceptions of Personal Capabilities, (4) Perceptions of Personal Significance, (5) Perceptions of Personal Influence, (6) Self-Discipline, (7) Interpersonal Skills, (8) Responsibility, (9) Judgmental Skills, (10) Social Inoculation, (11) Restructuring Relationships and (12) Working Together. These tapes are used in the Developing Capable People courses designed to help parents and teachers work more effectively with young people. (Sunrise Press, Fair Oaks, CA) Price: $49.95. **Order #T101** (Wt. 2 lbs.)

Bridging Troubled Waters by H. Stephen Glenn is a two-tape audio cassette on building bridges of

103

communication with adolescents. On these tapes, Steve examines barriers to parent/adolescent communications and suggests constructive skills to build positive communication. (Sunrise Press, Fair Oaks, CA, 1989) Price: $16.95. **Order #T102** (Wt. 1 lb.)

Involving and Motivating People by H. Stephen Glenn. Not many have heard Steve role play an outhouse builder resisting a drill salesman, or describe a creative way to deal with an angry neighbor ready to kill a resourceful horse. A fun way to learn essential principles that can improve relationships at home, school or work. (Sunrise Press, Fair Oaks, CA) Price: $10.00. **Order #T103** (Wt. 1 lb.)

Positive Discipline by Jane Nelsen is a 90- minute lecture to parents that makes Positive Discipline come alive. Everything on the tape can be found in the *Positive Discipline* book. It helps to hear a verbal reminder periodically by popping the tape into your car cassette deck. (Sunrise Press, Fair Oaks, CA) Price: $10.00. **Order #T104** (Wt. 1 lb.)

Positive Discipline in the Classroom: Featuring Class Meetings by Jane Nelsen. Jane Nelsen presents an all-day workshop to 500 teachers, including activities and role playing. A highlight of the workshop is a segment where Kay Rogers and Janice Ritter (two teachers who have experienced incredible success with class meetings) join Jane to answer questions on class meetings. Janice Ritter shares: "When we first started class meetings in our school, my initial reaction was, 'Well, this is a terrific idea, but it's not going to fly with first graders.' By December I said, 'This is the most wonderful thing that has ever happened to me as a teacher and for the students'." (Sunrise Press, Fair Oaks, CA, 1992) Price: $49.95. Order **#T108** (Wt. 3 lbs.)

Building Self-Esteem through Positive Discipline by Jane Nelsen provides guidelines for building self-esteem by using positive discipline principles. Children deserve to be treated with dignity and respect; this tape tells you how. (Sunrise Press, Fair Oaks, CA, 1994) Price: $10. Order **#T109** (Wt. 1 lb.)

Empowering Teenagers and Yourself In The Process by Jane Nelsen and Lynn Lott. This six-tape set was taken from a live workshop of the same title. The set includes a 109-page workbook so you can follow along with the participants and complete the activities to apply skills to your personal situations. The purpose of this workshop is to give adults the skills to educate, challenge and support our young people; to reaffirm ourselves—that we are worthwhile and so are our kids; to stop doing the things that don't work—like overcriticism, overambition, overindulgence, overprotection; to learn what *does* work to help

105

promote healthy attitudes and healthy behaviors. (Sunrise Press, Fair Oaks, CA, 1991) Price: $49.95 **Order #T113** (Wt. 3 lbs.); Study Guide only: Price: $9.95. **Order #M110** (Wt. 1 lb.)

VIDEOS BY H. STEPHEN GLENN AND JANE NELSEN

Positive Discipline by Jane Nelsen. These two one-hour videos show Jane presenting an overview of her Positive Discipline program. A *Positive Discipline Study Guide*, which allows for personal application, is included. The Study Guide can also be purchased separately for use with the *Positive Discipline* book or 90-minute cassette tape. (Sunrise Press, Fair Oaks, CA, 1988) Price: $49.95. **Order #V101** (Wt. 3 lbs.) Study Guide only: Price: $6.00. **Order #M107** (Wt. 1 lb.)

Developing Healthy Self-Esteem by H. Stephen Glenn. This video discusses the difference between high self-esteem and healthy self-esteem. It points out weaknesses in many popular approaches to self-esteem and suggests an alternative model that emphasizes self-respect and self-actualization (60 minutes). (Sunrise Productions, Fair Oaks, CA, 1989) Price: $39.95. **Order #V107** (Wt. 1 lb.)

Teachers Who Make A Difference by H. Stephen Glenn. This video begins with a special story of a teacher with an unusual gift for empowering
106

students as learners and then proceeds to identify and discuss five essential principles of empowerment in teaching (90 minutes). (Sunrise Productions, Fair Oaks, CA, 1989) Price: $49.95. **Order #V108** (Wt. 1 lb.)

Developing Capable People Videos by H. Stephen Glenn. This four-video set is an invaluable resource for anyone who works with young people—parents, teachers, counselors. The videos teach the key concepts in the Developing Capable People Course and provide a wealth of information about dealing effectively with young people and turning control over to them as soon as possible so they have power over their own lives. Topics include: social and lifestyle changes that have affected the ability of home and school to develop self-discipline, judgment, responsibility and other life skills in young people; the significant seven perceptions and skills; the five common behaviors that reduce closeness and trust; the greatest human need; and six steps to developing responsibility. (Four video set) (Sunrise Productions, Fair Oaks, CA, 1989) Price: $135. **Order #V114** (Wt. 5 lbs.)

MANUALS FOR FACILITATORS OF COURSES FOR PARENTS AND TEACHERS

Teaching Parenting by Lynn Lott and Jane Nelsen provides a step-by-step approach to starting and leading experientially based parenting groups.

Many parenting programs rely heavily on methods which provide excellent intellectual information and understanding. *Teaching Parenting* offers significant enhancement to any program through experiential activities and an "Empowering People Problem-Solving" process which reach the heart to inspire deeper understanding and change. These activities create the bridge to reach parents with cultural differences, limited reading skills and/or special problems with children. This program can be used alone or with a parenting book. Outlines are included for use with ten major parenting books. (Sunrise Press, Fair Oaks, CA, 1990) Price: $39.95. **Order #M106** (Wt. 3 lbs.)

Positive Discipline in the Classroom: Featuring Class Meetings Facilitator's Guide by Jane Nelsen and Lynn Lott. This manual is full of activities that can be used by teachers and students in the classroom, or for inservice training. Learn the Eight Building Blocks for Effective Class Meetings, other nonpunitive discipline methods and the Teachers Helping Teachers Problem-Solving Steps, where teachers learn to be consultants to each other and have fun role playing and brainstorming solutions. (Sunrise Press, Fair Oaks, CA, 1992) Price: $39.95 Order **#M113** (Wt. 3 lbs.)

Parenting in Recovery: The Next Step includes experiential activities to teach important concepts from every chapter of the book, *Clean and Sober*

Parenting. It can be used alone or in conjunction with the *Teaching Parenting* manual. (Sunrise Press, Fair Oaks, CA, 1992) Price: $19.95 Order **#M114** (Wt. 1 lb.)

Student Assistance through Positive Discipline by Steve Hageman, Lynn Lott and Jane Nelsen focuses on creating a Positive Discipline Student Assistance Program through the formation of a student intervention team, and is designed to be used with the *Positive Discipline in the Classroom Facilitator's Guide*. It is a manual for school personnel who are tired of spending too much of their time disciplining and who want collaboration and shared decision making to solve students problems. (Sunrise Press, Fair Oaks, CA, 1994) Price: $19.95 Order **#M115** (Wt. 1 lb.)

Positive Discipline for Single Parents Facilitator's Guide by Jane Nelsen and Cheryl Erwin contains thirty-eight activities developed especially for single parents. It includes an outline showing how to incorporate activities from the *Teaching Parenting* manual as well. (Sunrise Press, Fair Oaks, CA, 1994) Price: $19.95 Order **#M116** (Wt. 1 lb.)

Positive Discipline for Preschoolers Facilitator's Guide by Jane Nelsen, Cheryl Erwin and Roslyn Duffy contains activities developed especially for parents of preschoolers. It includes an outline showing how to incorporate activities from the *Teaching Parenting* manual as well. (Sunrise

109

Press, Fair Oaks, CA, 1994) Price: $19.95 Order **#M117** (Wt. 1 lb.)

OTHER RESOURCES

Songs for Elementary Emotional Development by Wayne Scott Frieden and Marie Hartwell-Walker. (Education Research Associates, Amherst, MA, 1982) The tape titled *Behavior Songs* includes a song for each of the Four Goals of Mistaken Behavior. Price: $8.00. **Order #T124** (Wt. 1 lb.) *Family Songs* includes delightful songs on seven birth order positions. Price: $8.00. **Order #T123** (Wt. 1 lb.)

SATISFACTION GUARANTEED!

(Prices subject to change without notice.)

To order, send this form to:

**EMPOWERING PEOPLE BOOKS, TAPES &
VIDEOS
P.O. BOX B
PROVO, UT 84603
1-800-456-7770**

Please send me:

Order #	Quantity	Title	Price

Total Price of Order   _____

Sales Tax: 7.25% (CA); 6.25% (UT)   _____

Shipping
(50¢ per lb. + $2.50 handling—Continental US) _____
($1 per lb. + $2.50 handling—Outside US)   _____

GRAND TOTAL (U.S. Funds only)   _____

Check enclosed _____

Charge my Visa_____ Mastercard_____
#_____ _____ _____ _____
Expires _____ / _____
Signature_____

Ship to:
Name_____
Address_____
City/State/Zip_____